GMAT Maths flashcards

Based on the tips of ALL the Quantitative (Maths) exercises in the Official GMAT book

✓ Useful to start preparing for GMAT

✓ No rocket science stuff: just what you need to know

✓ Ordered by topics

✓ In just 20 slides: don't trust long books (other than the official) or long and expensive lessons

✓ Prepared by a successful GMAT and MBA student in a top school

After understanding these tips and formulas... you can start doing exercises and exams!

KW-417-399

1

INDEX

- **Absolute values**
- **Areas and volumes**
- **Discounts**
- **Exponents**
- **Factors**
- **Gross profit**
- **Group problems**
- **Mixtures and solutions**
- **Multiples**
- **Odd / Even**
- **Percents**
- **Prime numbers**
- **Probability I**
- **Probability II**
- **Quadratics**
- **Work, rates, distances and speed**
- **Ratios**
- **Sum digits**
- **Triangles**
- **Other topics**

Absolute value

- Formulas to remember:
  - $|x|^2 = x^2$
  - $(|x + y|)^2 = (x + y)^2$
  - $|x| * |y| = |x * y|$
  - By definition of $|x|$, $|x| = x$ if $x \geq 0$ and $|x| = -x$ if $x < 0$

- Absolute value exercises like: How many solutions will this equation have? $|x+3| - |4-x| = |8+x|$ ---> we apply the "Critical Values" method for absolute values equations:

  - Step 1: do each absolute term equal to zero to obtain critical values. In the example, critical values are -3, 4, -8.

  - Step 2: place them in the Real numbers line to make all the possible intervals. Note that you have to include critical values in the intervals, that is why we put the term "less or equal" and "big or equal"... we put them as below by convention. In the example, the intervals (or conditions) are:

    - Condition 1: $x < -8$
    - Condition 2: $-8 \leq x < -3$
    - Condition 3: $-3 \leq x < 4$
    - Condition 4: $x \geq 4$

  - Step 3: set the predominant sign for each term under each condition, and solve the equation. In the example:

    - Condition 1: -(x+3) - (4-x) = -(8+x) → x = -1
    - Condition 2: -(x+3) - (4-x) = (8+x) → x = -15
    - Condition 3: (x+3) - (4-x) = (8+x) → x = 9
    - Condition 4: (x+3) + (4-x) = (8+x) → x = -1

  - Step 4: check if the solution satisfies the initial condition. In the example:

    - Condition 1: NO, -1 is not less than -8
    - Condition 2: NO, -15 is not between -8 and -3 (including -8 in the interval and not -3)
    - Condition 3: NO, 9 is not between -3 and 4 (including -3 in the interval and not 4)
    - Condition 4: NO, -1 is not equal or more than 4

  - Solution for the example: the initial equation does not have any solution.

- Absolute value exercises like: solve $|-3x+2|>7$:

  - There are two cases to study:
    - Case 1: (-3x+2)>7 → -3x>5 → x<(-5/3)
    - Case 2: -(-3x+2)>7 → 3x-2>7 → x>3

  - The solution is (-5/3)>x>3

3

Areas and volumes

- Circumferences:

  ○ $Perimeter = 2\pi r$

  ○ $Area = \pi r^2$

  ○ $Arc\ rR = \dfrac{x}{360} * perimeter$

  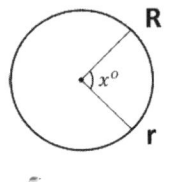

  ○ All triangles circumscribed in a circle, and with a side equal to the diameter D, will be right triangles

  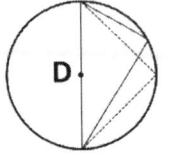

- Spheres:

  ○ $Volume = \dfrac{4}{3}\pi r^3$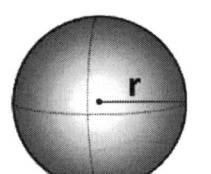

- Cones:

  ○ $Volume = \dfrac{1}{3}\pi r^2 * h$

  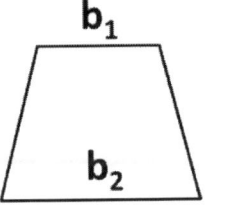

- Trapezoids:

  ○ $Area = \dfrac{(b_1 + b_2) * h}{2}$

4

Discounts

- If discount = n%, then:

  $$Price = \frac{(100 - n)}{100} * (original\ price)$$

- If you have to apply two discounts, remember always to apply first the first discount, and then the second i.e. do not try to calculate it very fast and in a single step: you can easily get confused. As you can see, there is no need to memorize the formulas below, as long as you understand the concepts. Formulas:

  $$Price\ with\ 1st\ discount = \frac{(100 - discount_1)}{100} * (original\ price)$$

  $$Price\ with\ 2nd\ discount = \frac{(100 - discount_2)}{100} * (price\ with\ 1st\ discount)$$

Exponents

- Formulas:

  o $x^r * y^r = (x * y)^r$

  o $x^{\frac{r}{s}} = \left(x^{\frac{1}{s}}\right)^r = \sqrt[s]{x^r}$

- Square roots:

  o   Properties:

     ▪ Exactly the same as explained above:
     $$x^r * y^r = (x * y)^r$$

     ▪ This means, for instance,
     $$\sqrt{A} * \sqrt{B} = \sqrt{A * B}$$

     ▪ Or, for example,
     $$\sqrt{2} * \sqrt{3} = \sqrt{6}$$

  o   Rationalization of the denominator:

     ▪ whenever we have a square root in the denominator, we "rationalize" to simplify the term. This is a mathematical convention used as well in GMAT.
     $$\frac{24}{\sqrt{3}}$$

     ▪ For example:

     ▪ Solution:
     $$\frac{24}{\sqrt{3}} * \frac{\sqrt{3}}{\sqrt{3}} = \frac{24 * \sqrt{3}}{3} = 8 * \sqrt{3}$$

6

Factors

- Note that common factors are always greater than 1.

  - Example: If you are asked the factors of 18, you should answer: 1, 2, 3, 6, 9, 18

  - Example: If you are asked the factors of 6, you should answer: 1, 2, 3, 6

- Greatest Common Factor of two numbers:

  - We decompose the two numbers in factors (factors that, by the way, are prime numbers) and select all common factors. Then, the "greatest common factor" is the result of multiplying those smaller common factors.

  - Example:

    - 135 = **5** x   **3** x **3** x 3

    - 225 = **5** x 5 x **3** x **3**

  - Solution: the "greatest common factor" is 45 (as 5 x 3 x 3 = 45).

- Lowest Common Multiple of two numbers:

  - We do the same decomposition. But now, we multiply all factors in either list. This means that if a factor is in both lists, we only pick it once... Look at the example below: the first 5 is in both lists, so we only pick one 5; the first and second 3 are in both lists, so we only pick them once; we add the second 5 (only in one list) and the third 3 (only in one list). The result is 5 x 5 x 3 x 3 x 3 = 675.

  - Example:

    - 135 = 5 x   **3** x **3** x **3**

    - 225 = **5** x **5** x 3 x 3

  - Solution: the "lowest common multiple" is 675 (as 5 x 5 x 3 x 3 x 3 = 675).

- Note: 13 x 7 = 91

Gross profit

- Gross profit = Selling price - Cost

- Gross profit = Revenues - Expenses

- Purchase price: typically, this means the Wholesaler price

- Market Value: typically, this means after markup

Group problems

- Group problems involving "Both/Neither":

    o Mixed group formula:

    Group1 + Group2 + Neither - Both = Total

- Group problems involving "Either/Or" categories (male/female, blue shirt/white shirt, etc.):

    o The best way is to organize the information into a grid.

    o Example: Among the employees of a certain company, 52 percent of the employees are male and 48 percent are female. In this company 70 percent of the male employees are married and 50 percent of the female employees are married. If one employee in the company is randomly selected, approximately what is the probability that he or she is NOT married?

	Male (52%)	Female (48%)
Married	70%	50%
Not Married	30%	50%

o Solution: the probability of picking one random person Not Married (he or she) is: 0.52 x 0.30 + 0.50 x 0.50 = 0.15 + 0.25 (approx.) Solution: 0.4 approximately.

- Set problem:

    o Example: Each of 200 people is enrolled in biology, math, or both. If 120 are enrolled in biology and 60 are enrolled in math, how many are enrolled in both?

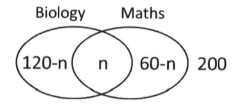

Biology   Maths

120-n (n) 60-n) 200

    o Solution: 200 = 120 - n + n + 60 - n

Mixtures and solutions

- Mixture problem:

  ○ $$(C_1) * (L_1) + (C_2) * (L_2) = (C_{Mixture}) * (L_1 + L_2)$$

  ○ Where,

    ▪ is the concentration of the solution 1

    ▪ is the concentration of the solution 2

    ▪ is the amount of liters of the solution 1

    ▪ is the amount of liters of the solution 2

    ▪ is the concentration of the whole mixture

  ○ Example: How many liters of a solution that is 12% salt must be added to 6 liters of a solution that is 9% salt so that the resulting mixture is 11% salt?

  ○ Solution:

  $$0.12 * L_1 + 0.09 * 6 = 0.11 * (L_1 + 6)$$

- Note: if the problem talks about evaporation, bear in mind that Sodium Chloride will never evaporate because it's a salt.

Multiples

- Multiples of 3:
  - the sum of the digits is multiple of 3.
- Multiples of 4:
  - OR last two digits are multiple of 4,
  - OR the number can be divided by 2 twice.
- Multiples of 6:
  - the number is multiple of 3 and 2.
- Multiples of 9:
  - the sum of the digits is multiple of 9.
- Multiples of 12:
  - check divisibility by 3, AND check divisibility by 4.

- Examples:
  - Is 900 multiple of 12? Yes, because the sum of the digits is multiple of 3 (12 x 75 = 900) AND the number can be divided by 2 twice.
  - Is 1512 multiple of 12? Yes, because the sum of the digits is multiple of 3 (1+5+1+2 = 9) AND the number can be divided by 2 twice.

Odds/Even

- Addition and subtraction: a MIX between odd and even is ODD:

  o ODD ± ODD = EVEN

  o EVEN ± EVEN = EVEN

  o ODD ± EVEN = ODD

- Multiplication: if there is an EVEN, the result is EVEN:

  o ODD x ODD = ODD

  o EVEN x EVEN = EVEN

  o ODD x EVEN = EVEN

- Other important rules:

  o ODD numbers only have ODD factors

  o ODD roots and exponents: always preserve the sign

- Consecutive integers formula:

  o EVEN: $2n, 2n+2, 2n+4...$

  o ODD: $2n+1, 2n+3, 2n+5...$

Percents

- $Percent\ increase = \dfrac{amount\ of\ change}{original\ amount}$

- $Portion = \dfrac{percent}{100} * Whole$

- Example:
  - 20 is 2/5 % of what number?
  - Solution:

$$20 = \frac{2}{5} * \frac{1}{100} * Whole$$

Prime numbers

- List of prime numbers from 1 to 100: 2, 3, 5, 7, 11, 13, 17, 19, 23, 29, 31, 37, 41, 43, 47, 53, 59, 61, 67, 71, 73, 79, 83, 89, 97.

- 1 is not prime

- 2 is the smallest and only even prime

- For all integers > 1:
  - OR is prime
  - OR can be expressed as a product of prime numbers

Probability (1)

- Rules of Probability:
  - 1st rule: Simple probability:
    $$P(A) = \frac{outcomes\ in\ A}{total\ outcomes}$$
  - 2nd rule:
    $$P(E) = 1 - P(not\ E)$$
  - 3rd rule:
    $$P(A\ and\ B) = P(A) \times P(A|B)$$
    - $P(A|B)$ is the probability of A given B
    - if A and B are two independent events (this is the typical GMAT case), then its simpler: $P(A\ and\ B) = P(A) \times P(B)$
  - 4th rule:
    $$P(A\ or\ B) = P(A) + P(B) - P(A\ and\ B)$$

- Other General Rules:
  - $P(A\ and\ B) < P(A\ or\ B)$
  - $P(A\ or\ B) > P(A)$
  - and similarly $P(A\ or\ B) > P(B)$

- Permutations:
  - In permutations, the order matters. Number of permutations of r objects from a set of n objects:
  - Formula: $P_r^n = \dfrac{n!}{(n-r)!}$
  - Note: if n=r, then $P_n^n = n!$. This applies, for instance, if the questions is: "count the number of ways that a set of n objects can be ordered"

- Indistinguishable events:
  - Distinct permutations with repeated items.
  - Formula: $\dfrac{n!}{r1! * r2! * \cdots * rk!}$
    - n is the number of items in the set
    - r1 is the number of repeated items of style 1
    - r2 is the number of repeated items of style 2
    - rk is the number of repeated items of style k
  - Example: how many different ways can the letters in the word TRUST be arranged?
    $$\frac{5!}{2!} = 60$$

  - Example: how many different six-digit numbers can be written using all of the following six digits: 9-9-9-7-7-8? $\dfrac{6!}{3! * 2!} = 60$

- Circular permutations:
  - The number of ways to arrange n distinct objects along a fixed circle is: $(n-1)!$

- Combinations:
  - In combinations, the order doesn't matter. If order of selection is not relevant and only r objects are able to be selected from a large set of n objects:
  - Formula: $C_r^n = \dfrac{n!}{r!\,(n-r)!} = \binom{n}{r}$

- Probability of choosing a random point within Y:
  - If a point is chosen at random within a space with an area, volume, or length of Y and a space with a respective area, volume, or length of X lies within Y, the probability of choosing a random point within Y is the area, volume, or length of X divided by the area, volume, or length of Y.
  - Therefore, solution is always $\dfrac{X}{Y}$

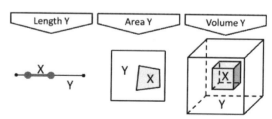

Probability (and 2)

- Other formulas:

  o If A can be chosen in m ways, and B can be chosen in n ways. To choose both A and B there are m·n ways.

  o If there are n outcomes when running an experiment, and we run the experiment m times, there will be n^m possible outcomes. Example: a coin flipped 8 times: there are 2^8 possible outcomes.

- Average (mean): $mean = \sum_{1}^{n} \frac{x_i}{n}$

- Median:

  o if n is odd: order the numbers from least to greatest - do not disregard repeated numbers -, then select the number in the middle of the list

  o if n is even: order the numbers from least to greatest - do not disregard repeated numbers -, then select the two numbers in the middle of the list and make the average of them

- Mode: most frequent numbers in a list. Note that many numbers can meet this rule: select all of them

- Range: greatest number minus the smallest

- Standard deviation:

$$std\ dev = \sqrt{\frac{\sum_{1}^{n}(mean - x_i)^2}{n}}$$

Quadratics

- $(x + y)^2 = x^2 + y^2 + 2xy$

- $(x - y)^2 = x^2 + y^2 - 2xy$

- $(x + y)(x - y) = x^2 - y^2$

  o And obvious but useful to remember: given y=1,
$$(x + 1)(x - 1) = x^2 - 1$$

Work, rates, distances and speed

- Distances & speed exercises: they look easy, but you want to remember them when facing an exercise of this type:

  ○ $$Average\ speed = \frac{Total\ distance}{Total\ time}$$

  ○ **Distance**$= Rate * Time$

- Work problems:

  ○ Previous notes before the formula:

    ▪ Let 1 A (A=machine, man, woman...) complete the job in "a" days and 1 B (B=machine, man, woman...) in "b" days.

    ▪ the rate of 1 A is $\frac{1}{a}$ job/days (rate of 1 A)

    ▪ the rate of 1 B is $\frac{1}{b}$ job/days (rate of 1 B)

  ○ The formula to get the total time "t" if they work together is:

  $$\frac{1}{t} = \frac{1}{a} + \frac{1}{b}$$

  ○ Other key formula:

  $$Rate = \frac{Job}{Time}$$

○ Example 1 on how to use the formula: Mary can paint the wall in 3 days, while John can paint the wall in 5 days; how many days will it take to paint the wall if they work together?

  ▪ $$\frac{1}{t} = \frac{1}{3} + \frac{1}{5}$$

○ Example 2 on how to use the formula: It takes 6 days for 3 women and 2 men working together to complete a work:

  ▪ $$\frac{1}{6} = \frac{3}{w} + \frac{2}{m}$$

○ Example 3 on how to use this logic: 3 men would do the same work 5 days sooner than 9 women:

  ▪ $$\frac{m}{3} + 5 = \frac{w}{9}$$

  ▪ $$\frac{1}{m} + \frac{1}{w} = \frac{1}{t}$$

○ Example 4 on how to use this logic: 1 men would do the same work 5 days sooner than 1 women:

  ▪ $$m + 5 = w$$

  ▪ $$\frac{1}{m} + \frac{1}{w} = \frac{1}{t}$$

Ratios

- A ratio is expressed as: **Ratio of a to b** $= \frac{a}{b}$

  ○ Example: **Ratio of 2 to 5** $= \frac{2}{5}$

- Ratio of a to b can be written also as a:b

- Inverse ratio of a:b is b:a (also called Reciprocal ratio since b:a = 1/a : 1/b

- If an amount is divided between A and B in the ratio a: b, then:

  ○ **A share** $= \frac{a}{a+b}$

  ○ **B share** $= \frac{b}{a+b}$

    ▪ Example: If \$936 are divided between worker A and worker B in the ratio 5: 7,what is the share that worker B will get?

    ▪ Solution: The ratio a:b is 5:7, and therefore the share of B will be

    B share $= \frac{b}{a+b}$ or

    B share $= \frac{7}{5+7} = 0.5833$

▪ The exam can ask for the percentage solution (i.e. 58.33%) or for the unitary/monetary solution (i.e. 58.33% of 936\$=546\$ approx.)

Sum digits

- In this type of exercises, you are given an addition similar or like the one below, where AB and CD are 2 digit numbers and EFG is a 3 digit number (all digits are positive numbers i.e. none is zero). Typically, you have to come up with the value of F for example. In the points below we give some hints to solve these questions:

$$
\begin{array}{r}
A\,B \\
+\quad C\,D \\
\hline
E\,F\,G
\end{array}
$$

1. As the sum of two numbers with two digits can never be bigger than 198 (99+99=198), always E=1

2. G = unit digit of (B+D)

3. F = unit digit of (A+C) + tens digit of (B+D)

- Example 1: AB + CD = AAA, where AB and CD are 2 digit numbers and AAA is a 3 digit number. A,B,C and D are distinct positive numbers. In the above addition problem, what is the value of C? Solution:

  o A=1 (see hint number 1 above), therefore AAA=111

  o B + D cannot sum 1 (as both B and D are positive digits), therefore they must sum 11

  o Note there are multiple combinations for B and D, as B+D =11

  o C must be 9. Solution: C=9

- Example 2: BA + AB = CDC, where BA and AB are 2 digit numbers and CDC is a 3 digit number. A,B,C and D are distinct positive numbers. In the above addition problem, what is the value of A? Solution:

  o C=1 (see hint number 1 above), therefore CDC=1D1

  o B + A cannot sum 1 (as both B and A are positive digits), therefore they must sum 11. A + B must also sum 11

  o D must be 2

  o Solution: there are multiple solutions for A (A=7 and B=4; A=4 and B=7; A=8 and B=3...) as long as A+B=11

Triangles

- Properties of RIGHT triangles:

  ○ $X^2 + Y^2 = Z^2$

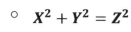

  ○ Typical values for right triangle sides:
    - 3-4-5
    - 5-12-13
    - 9-12-15

  ○ Right triangle 30-60-90:

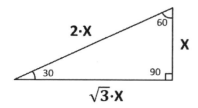

  ○ Right triangle 45-45-90:

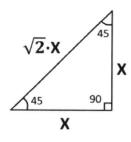

- Properties for all kind of triangles:

  ○ For all triangles: Sum of angles is always = 180º

  ○ Note: for a polygon of N sides - e.g. N=3 for a triangle -, the sum of angles is always = 180·(N-2)

  ○ For all triangles, the formulas below apply:
    - X + Y > Z
    - X + Z > Y
    - Y + Z > X

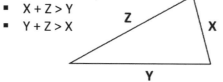

- Other things to remember:

  ○ $\sqrt{2} \approx 1.41$

  ○ $\sqrt{3} \approx 1.73$

  ○ $\pi \approx \dfrac{22}{7} \approx 3.1415$

- Properties for angles inside a circumference:

  ○ $minor\ arc = 2 * inscribed\ angle$

    - where β is the minor arc,
    - α is the inscribed angle,
    - and D is the diameter

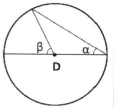

- Similar triangles and areas: the ratio of the areas of two similar triangles is the square of the ratio of corresponding lengths:

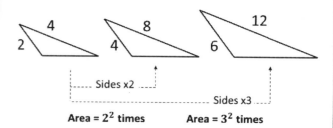

- Other triangle properties:

  ○ $d = a + b$

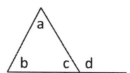

Other topics

- About integers:

  o Recall that integers can be positive, negative, or zero: ... -2, -1, 0, 1, 2 ...

  o Count integers: number of integers from A to B inclusive: B - A + 1

  o Consecutive integers:
    - Sum of consecutive integers = average x number of terms
    - Average of a set of evenly spaced consecutive integers = average of smallest and largest numbers in the set = median

  o Number added or deleted to a set of numbers:
    - Total = mean x number of terms
    - Number added or deleted = |original total - new total|

- Properties of zero:
  o Is an EVEN integer
  o Is not positive, neither negative
  o Is a factor of no number
  o Is multiple of all numbers
  o Factorial of zero is 1: $0! = 1$

- Fraction properties:

  o $y = x * q + r$

  o $x > r$

  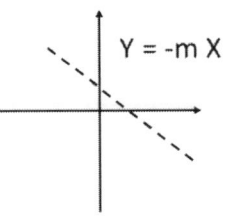

  o where:
    - Y is the dividend
    - X is the divisor
    - q is the quotient
    - r is the remainder

- Slopes:

  o The slope can be calculated with two points of a line: $m = \dfrac{y_2 - y_1}{x_2 - x_1}$

  o Negative slope:

  Y = -m X

  o Positive slope:

  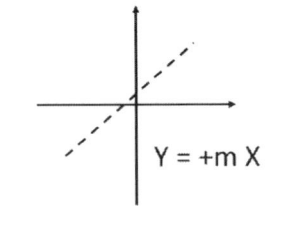

  Y = +m X

- Reciprocal of a number:
  $number * reciprocal = number * \dfrac{1}{number} = 1$

- 1 foot = 12 inches

22

Your personal notes

Your personal notes

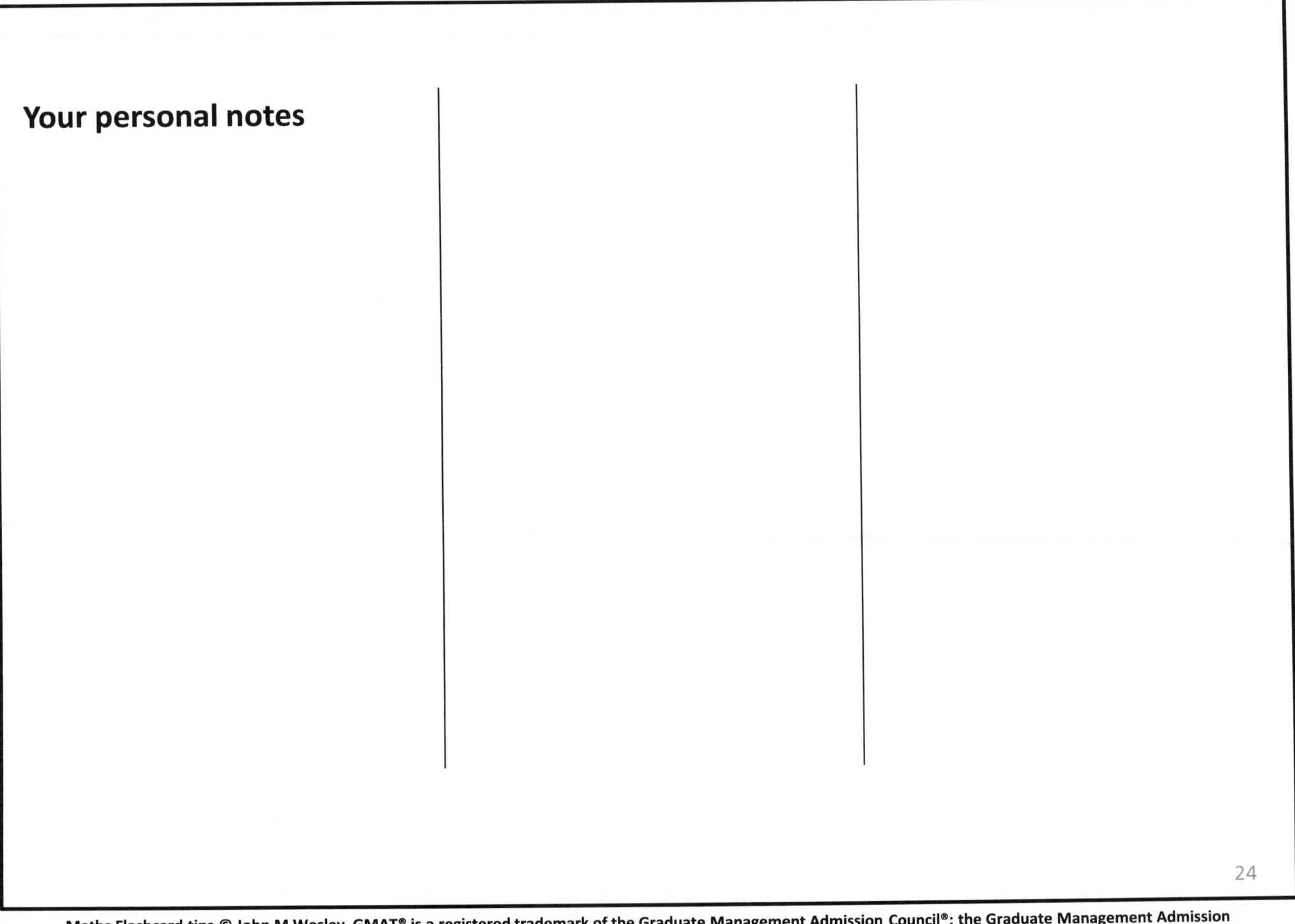

24

Your personal notes

Your personal notes

Printed in Great Britain
by Amazon.co.uk, Ltd.,
Marston Gate.